Technology in the Time of
The Maya

Judith Crosher

RSVP
RAINTREE
STECK-VAUGHN
PUBLISHERS
The Steck-Vaughn Company

Austin, Texas

Titles in the series

Ancient Egypt   **The Aztecs**

Ancient Greece   **The Maya**

Ancient Rome   **The Vikings**

Cover picture: A Mayan builder cutting limestone with a flint ax
Title page: A statuette of a woman weaving on a backstrap loom

Consultant: Elizabeth Carmichael, Museum of Mankind

© Copyright 1998, text, Steck-Vaughn Company

Published by Raintree Steck-Vaughn Publishers,
an imprint of Steck-Vaughn Company

Library of Congress Cataloging-in-Publication Data
Crosher, Judith.
Technology in the time of the Maya / Judith Crosher.
    p.   cm.
    Includes bibliographical references and index.
    ISBN 0-8172-4881-1
    1. Mayas—Industries—Juvenile literature.
    2. Mayas—Material culture—Juvenile literature.
    3. Mayas—Antiquities—Juvenile literature.
    4. Central America—Antiquities—Juvenile literature.
    5. Mexico—Antiquities—Juvenile literature.
    I. Title.
F1435.3.I53C76   1997
609.72—dc21   97-24119

Printed in Italy. Bound in the United States.
1 2 3 4 5 6 7 8 9 0 02 01 00 99 98

Contents

Introduction

The Mayan people have lived in Central America for thousands of years. Their ancient civilization reached its peak between A.D. 250 and A.D. 925, when the Maya made some remarkable advances in technology. At this time, the Maya were a Stone Age people; that is, they had no metal. Nor did they have plows, wheels, or pack animals. In spite of this, their farmers were able to grow enough food to support an aristocracy who lived in magnificent palaces.

Chichen Itza Temple

The Maya built temples and huge cities in the mountains and rain forests of Central America.

Using simple tools of flint and wood, the Maya built huge stone pyramids and temples. They made elegant, painted pottery and carved one of the hardest stones, jade, into delicate jewelry. They made gorgeous costumes out of wicker, feathers, and richly decorated cloth. Their astronomers calculated the movements of the sun, moon, and planets, developed a more efficient system of arithmetic than the Romans, and created a calendar with a cycle of 5,128 years. They made libraries of books on medicine, history, nature, and religion. In this book you can see the tools and technology the Maya used to create this civilization.

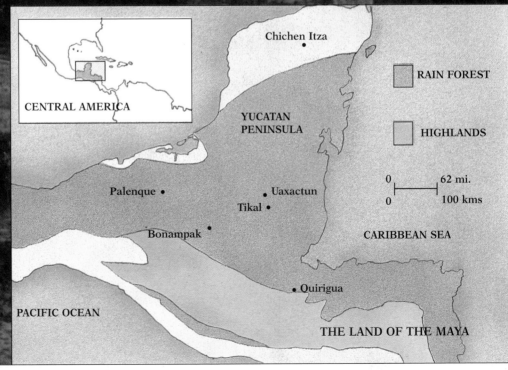

CENTRAL AMERICA

Chichen Itza

RAIN FOREST

YUCATAN
PENINSULA

HIGHLANDS

Palenque

Uaxactun
Tikal

0   62 mi.
0   100 kms

Bonampak

CARIBBEAN SEA

Quirigua

PACIFIC OCEAN

THE LAND OF THE MAYA

Farming

Armed only with wooden digging sticks and stone-bladed hoes and axes, the Maya farmed several different kinds of land. Historians once thought that Mayan farming was a simple process. The Maya cut down forests in the autumn, burned it in the winter, planted seeds before the spring rains, and then moved on to a new section of forest. This was true only in the highlands, which had deep soil and regular rainfall. It was harder in the dry Yucatan to the north, with its thin layer of soil. There the Maya had to build thousands of cisterns lined with plaster, to catch and store rain.

Drainage Canals

The swampy central lowlands posed a different problem. The National Aeronautics and Space Administration (NASA) discovered how Mayan farmers were able to grow enough to feed up to eight million people. Photographs taken from space show an incredible network of drainage canals weaving through the wet land. Farmers dug earth from these canal beds and piled it up, creating raised fields of soft, fertile soil.

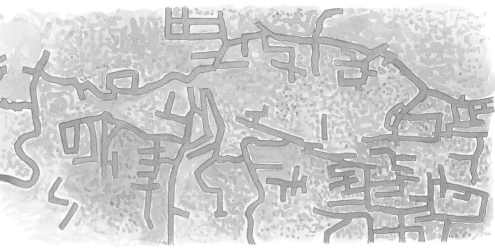

Planting Corn

This picture from an ancient Mayan book, or "codex" shows a farmer making a hole with his digging stick and dropping in corn seeds. Some furrowed fields have survived, perfectly preserved beneath ash from a volcanic eruption. They show that the Maya planted corn on ridges, with beans and squash in the furrows.

Cenotes

In the Yucatan region, rainwater seeped through the limestone soil into huge, natural underground wells called *cenotes*. The Maya built long ladders of logs tied together with ropes made of twisted vines, so that they could reach and collect this water.

Ikat Patterns

The Maya used some plants to dye food and thread. The thread was dyed, tied into yarn, and then woven, to create blurred patterns. You can create similar patterns using tie-dye. You will need cotton cloth, pebbles, string, and dye.

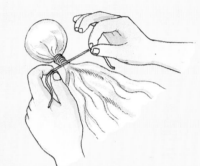

1 Place a pebble in the cloth and tie it with string. This keeps the dye from coloring that part of the cloth. Tie in as many pebbles as you wish.

2 Dye your cloth, following the instructions on the package.

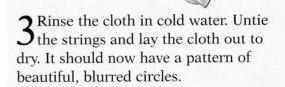

3 Rinse the cloth in cold water. Untie the strings and lay the cloth out to dry. It should now have a pattern of beautiful, blurred circles.

Hunting and Fishing

For meat, the Maya bred turkeys, doves, and a kind of barkless dog. They hunted deer, tapir, and peccary in the forests, tracking them with dogs and bringing them down with slingshots or *atlatls,* which fired darts. Jaguar, tapir, deer, and armadillo were trapped in deep pits covered with light branches. To obtain beautiful feathers from birds like the bright green quetzal, Mayan hunters shot them with darts fired from blowpipes.

Fishing

On the coast, fishermen used bone hooks on lines, or big dragnets weighed down with stones like the one used by this modern-day Maya. Inland, they built dams on small rivers to create a pool. When enough fish swam into the pool, the fishermen would drop in a crushed, poisonous root of the balche tree. Then they picked out the fish, which had been paralyzed by the poison.

Snares

Mayan hunters used rope woven from plant fibers to make snares.

1 The hunters found a path used by animals going to a watering hole and dug a shallow trench along it, next to a springy sapling. They drove in a straight stake on one side of the trench and a stake with a crooked top on the other side.

2 They then tied one end of a long piece of rope to the top of the young tree and made a noose in its other end. Above the noose, they tied a stick long enough to stretch between the two stakes.

3 The hunters bent the tree over and attached the stick lightly between the two stakes so that the noose hung over the trench. They scattered leaves on the ground to hide their footprints.

4 When an animal ran along the trench, it put its head through the noose and dislodged the cross-stick. The tree recoiled, jerking the animal into the air and strangling it. This picture from a codex shows a Mayan hunter armed with a spear. A deer that he has caught in a snare is tied to his back.

Preparing Food

One of the Maya's most important discoveries was the *nixtamal* technique for treating corn, which was their staple diet. Before grinding corn, they boiled it with white lime or ground-up snail shells. This improved the balance of amino acids and allowed the body to absorb a chemical called niacin from the grain. It sounds like a simple process, but without it the Mayan civilization might not have developed. Without niacin, people would have died of pellagra, a vitamin deficiency that makes your skin peel off.

The Maya's only source of sugar was honey. The bees of Central America have no sting, and Mayan farmers kept them in hollow logs plugged with mud at either end and stacked up in a frame of poles.

Grinding corn

1 To prepare corn, a woman used a *tapiscadore* made of deer bone or wood to scrape the edible kernels from the husk. She held the cob pointing away from her and pushed the tool down each row, splitting off the kernels.

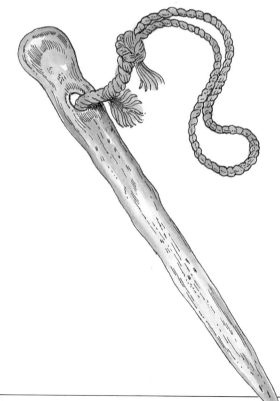

2 The stone slab (*metate*) and rolling pin (*mano*) with which a Mayan cook ground her corn every morning were carefully designed. The slab stood on three legs to keep it from wobbling on uneven ground and sloped away from the worker to make her job easier. This picture shows a pottery figure of a woman grinding corn using a metate and mano.

Nonstick Pans

Many traditional Mayan techniques are still used today. This woman is making the traditional clay dish in which thin, flat corn cakes called tortillas are cooked. After shaping the flat round tray, the potter rubs it over with a coat of fine clay mixed with ground talc and water. When it is dry, she polishes this coating with a smooth stone to create a nonstick surface.

Making Tortillas

People in Mayan households cooked batches of tortillas every morning. You can make tortillas using 8 oz. (230 g) flour, 2 oz. (60 g) lard, 1 teaspoon of salt, and 4 oz. (125 ml) warm water. Using a large mixing bowl, rub the lard into the flour with your fingers. Dissolve the salt in the water and add to the bowl. Knead for ten minutes. Divide the mixture into balls of 1.5 in. (4 cm) diameter. Cover each with flour, and use a rolling pin to roll it into a thin circle. Place each circle carefully in a heated frying pan. Cook for 20 seconds on each side. Serve with a sauce of chopped tomatoes, onions, and lime juice.

Building

Cities

The Maya designed their cities as a series of open plazas or squares. Around these they built stone platforms of different heights. A survey at Tikal has shown that all the horizontal surfaces of the buildings and the plaza were built with a slight slope, which guided precious rainwater to the city's reservoirs.

In the suburbs, ordinary families built two-roomed houses on low mounds of beaten earth and rubble. The remains of these platforms show that cities like Tikal housed up to 90,000 people. Houses were made of whatever was available: stone, mud bricks dried in the sun, or wooden poles woven together and filled with mud. The walls were covered with thick, white limestone plaster, and the roofs were thatched with palm leaves.

Building Cities

Instead of pulling down city platforms when they wanted to rebuild, the Maya built up and over them. You can see here how, as the city of Uaxactun became richer, this group of temples and palaces grew and developed.

Making Limestone Plaster

The Maya needed tons of plaster to decorate their buildings. They required huge amounts of logs and limestone to make it, using the following technique.

1 The Mayan builders stacked a pile of logs 5 ft. (1.5 m) high in a circle. They left a hole 12 in. (30 cm) wide in the middle. On top they heaped a layer of crushed limestone 30 in. (80 cm) high.

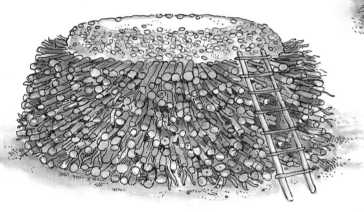

2 They dropped leaves and rotten wood into the center and set it on fire. It burned for about 36 hours, from the bottom up and from the inside out. This left a pile of powdered quicklime.

3 When the builders were ready to plaster, the quicklime was mixed with water, or "slaked," and left to become gluey. As it dried, the mixture became calcium carbonate, which made a hard, smooth, and long-lasting plaster.

The Firestick

The only light in a Mayan house came from the fire. Like other ancient people, the Maya made fire by twirling a stick of hard wood between their hands in a hole in a piece of softer wood. They placed dry leaves or moss next to the hole to catch the sparks. This picture from a codex shows two gods using a firestick.

Temples, Palaces, and Tombs

The Maya built temples at the top of pyramids formed from a series of platforms. Their core was made by heaping up rubble. Mayan builders covered this with an outer layer of stone blocks. In the highlands they used sandstone or volcanic rock. In the west there was no stone, so they made and fired clay bricks. The lowland Maya were lucky to have so much limestone. It is a soft stone, easily cut with simple flint blades and hammers. After limestone has been exposed to the air it becomes much harder.

Cutting Stone

The temple pyramids were remarkable works of technology for a people who had only simple tools. The Maya cut the huge stone blocks needed to build them using axes with blades made from flint.

The Temple of the Inscriptions

The Temple of the Inscriptions was built at Palenque around A.D. 800. In 1949, an archaeologist noticed some filled-in holes in a slab in the temple floor. He realized they had held ropes to lower the slab into place. For three years, his workers dug out rubble from a hidden stairway beneath the slab, down through the pyramid to an underground tomb. Inside was a sarcophagus covered with a stone lid weighing 12,100 pounds (5,500 kg).

Corbel Vaults

The Maya wanted to build stone roofs on their temples in the same shape as thatched roofs, but did not know how to make arches. The corbel vault solved this problem, but reduced the size of the room beneath and was quite unstable.

1 The builder laid a row of stones on a strong wall, with their edges slightly inside the edge. The next row of stones overlapped even more. To keep the stones from falling off, he put another layer over their back ends.

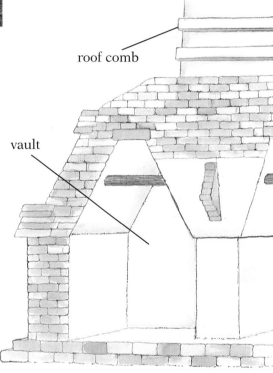

roof comb

vault

2 As the builder went on, he had to weigh down each overlapping layer in the same way. Halfway up he put a log across to strengthen the vault. At the top, he laid a large stone. On top of the temple he built two walls, joined with a wooden cross-tie. The weight of this "roof comb" helped counterbalance the temple wall against the pressure of the vault.

Decoration

The white plastered houses and churches that you see in Central America follow a tradition of decoration that stretches back more than 2,000 years. The Maya coated the inside and outside walls, platforms, and steps of their buildings with plaster.

The construction techniques the Maya used meant there was not much room inside their buildings. Public rituals were held outside, in the great plazas or on temple platforms. So the outsides of buildings were important—they were like the backdrop on a stage. As priests performed their ceremonies, behind them the people could see huge molded and painted images of their kings and gods.

Stucco Portraits

This head of a priest decorated the roof comb of a temple. It was made from a thick, molded plaster called stucco. The builder drew the outline of the head on the white plaster wall. He then built up layer after layer of plaster to make the features of the face.

Painting a Fresco

The Maya used the same technique to decorate pots like this one as they did to paint frescos on temple walls. The painter applied two layers of white plaster, which made a perfect background for brilliant colors. He then drew the outline of the picture, using an animal-hair brush that held a lot of paint—important for porous surfaces. He placed a third layer of plaster over part of the outline. While it was still wet, the painter redrew the outline and quickly filled in the colors. As the paint dried it became part of the plaster.

The Maya's favorite pigments were red iron oxide from anthills, brown and yellow ocher, a blue clay called attapulgite, black charcoal, and white chalk.

Painting a Pot

Try Mayan painting using a terra-cotta flowerpot, plaster of Paris, and a Chinese brush. The Maya used natural pigments mixed with water and resin to make a slightly transparent paint. You can use powder paint mixed with beaten egg white.

1 Cover the pot with a coat of plaster of Paris mixed with water, to create a white background. Let it dry.

2 Paint borderlines around the top and bottom, and add some "glyphs" like those along the right side and top of the pot pictured above.

3 With brown paint and the tip of your brush, outline your picture with a fine line. You could copy the design from the pot above. Now color it in.

Latex

The Spanish who invaded Central America in the sixteenth century were amazed by the rubber balls the Maya used: "When they hit the ground, they gather energy so that even if they are struck softly they jump right up into the sky with an incredible bounce." The Spanish had never seen rubber before.

The Maya called the rubber tree *cahuchu*, which means "weeping wood." When the bark is cut it oozes milky, white latex. They dried this latex to burn as incense or shaped it in molds to make a large, solid ball. This was used in a ball game that was both a sport and a religious ritual. Every city had at least one ball court, a vast, stone arena with sloping sides against which players had to bounce the huge rubber ball.

Ball Game

This stone marker from a ball game shows a player hitting the rubber ball, which weighed more than 6 pounds (3kg). The player wears a padded, wooden body yoke and an elaborate headdress. The leather guards stuffed with cotton on one knee, foot, and wrist protected him when he threw himself at the ball. The player had to keep the ball in the air by hitting it with his arms, waist, or thigh. He could score a goal by rebounding the ball onto this stone marker, which was laid on the ground.

Incense Burners

The valuable resin of the copal tree was called *pom*. The Maya shaped it into little cakes, painted them blue, and burned them in sculpted incense-holders, like the one below, during religious ceremonies. Painters mixed *pom* with their pigments to make the colors shiny and to help the paint stick to the surface of pots.

Rubber Tapping

The Maya cut V-shaped slits in the bark of various trees to drain off their sap or latex. One of the most useful trees was the sapodilla. Ants did not eat its wood, so Mayan builders used it for door lintels. Its sweet fruit was high in vitamin C. The Maya also boiled the latex that oozed from the sapodilla and used it as chewing gum.

Ball Game

The Mayan ball game was complex and dangerous. You can play a safe, simple version if there is a high wall without windows in your playground. First ask permission. Use chalk to draw a box on the ground 10 ft. (3 m) x 10 ft. (3 m), 3 ft. (1 m) away from the wall. Play the game with a light volleyball. Player A serves underarm from behind the box, striking the ball with one hand. The ball must hit the wall and rebound into the box. After one bounce, Player B strikes the ball so that it hits the wall and rebounds into the box. The rally continues until one player misses the wall or box, or allows the ball to bounce twice. Their opponent then scores one point. Take turns serving. The first player to reach ten points wins.

Spinning and Weaving

Ropes and Baskets

The mats and baskets that the Maya used have rotted away in the heat and damp. We can tell how they were made by looking at the few fragments that are left and the techniques of present-day Maya who work in traditional ways. Mayan carvings and paintings show us what they made from rushes and plant fibers: ropes for making snares, tying sandals, and hauling limestone blocks; dyed and woven mats; and light, strong baskets and bags.

The strongest fiber came from the agave plant. Its leaves were pounded into pulp, soaked for a few days, and then scraped off. This left a triangular mass of fibers, which was washed, combed, and hung up to dry.

Making String

1 To make string, the spinner first ties a few of the dried agave fibers around the arrow-shaped notch in a paddle like the one shown below.

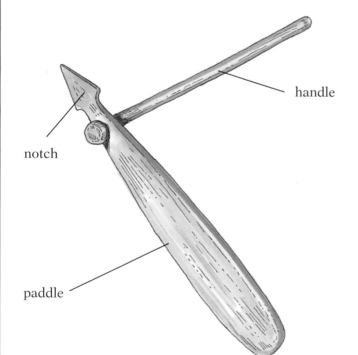

handle

notch

paddle

2 Holding a handle in each hand, the spinner walks backward from the agave bundle, spinning the paddles counterclockwise to twist the fibers. A helper feeds out the fibers. Once she has made two lengths of string, each about 20 ft. (6 m) long, the girl twists them together, this time spinning in a clockwise direction.

Basket Weaving

This modern Mayan basket-maker has tied a cord tightly around the middle of a bundle of thin canes and splayed them out in a circle. He then bends them upright to make the sides, and weaves rushes in and out. Finally, he weaves in brightly colored feathers to make a pattern around the rim.

Weaving a Basket

To make a Mayan basket, you will need 40 long straws, string, and colored cotton or feathers.

1 Tie the string tightly around the middle of 20 straws. Bend the bottom half of each straw up and the top half down, so the ends all stick out in a circle.

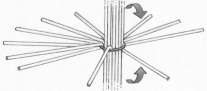

2 Bend up the two ends of each straw about 4 in. (10 cm) from the center, to form the sides.

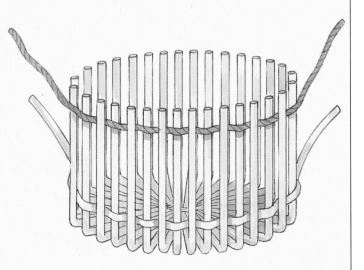

3 Weave in the remaining straws, cutting and sticking them together when the ends meet. At the top of the basket, you can weave in the colored cotton or feathers to create a pattern.

Spindles and Looms

Ancient Mayan paintings and sculptures show people wearing cloth decorated with bright, complicated patterns. However, they cannot tell us whether these patterns were woven into the cloth or embroidered on later. Only a few tiny scraps of cloth are left—the rest have rotted away. We do know that the Maya wore cotton, grown in the lowlands, and wove it on a backstrap loom in the same way as present-day Maya.

Spinning Cotton

To prepare cotton for spinning, the girl on the right beats it on a hard leather cushion to separate the fibers. The spinner pulls the fibers from a bundle in her left hand. She must be gentle or the fragile fibers will break. With her other hand, she twists her spindle, resting it in a gourd. The Maya dyed the spun cotton, then dipped it in a mixture of corn and water to give it a smooth coating of starch. This made it easier to weave.

Backstrap Loom

Today, the Maya still weave cloth on the traditional backstrap loom. This simple and efficient loom stretches between a pair of two meter-long rods, and was the result of much thought and experiment.

The weaver turns the sword-shaped **batten** on its side, holding the warp threads apart. This allows her to thread through the shuttle carrying the horizontal, or "weft," threads. She weaves at one end, then stops and begins at the other. This keeps the warp from tangling when she takes the loom down for the day.

The weaver has tied one loom rod to a tree and slipped the **backstrap** of the other rod around her hips. Leaning forward or back makes the warp threads looser or tighter.

The vertical, or "warp," threads were created first, when the weaver wound her yarn in a "figure eight" around two sticks. She has taken this off the sticks, slid a cord through each end, and lashed them to a **loom rod**. These lashings become part of the cloth, making a strong edge.

The backstrap loom shown on this pottery figure made in A.D. 700 looks just like the modern one above. When she had completed the weft threads, the weaver cut the lashings off the rods. The cloth was now ready to be sewn.

Clothing

The Maya never cut their cloth. A weaver decided what she wanted to make, then wove her cloth to the exact size. A woman wore a white petticoat beneath a *huipil,* a straight dress sewn up the sides with holes left for neck and arms. A man wore a narrow sash wound around his hips and between his legs, with the ends hanging down. A square of cloth made a cloak. Ceremonial costume included fantastic headdresses made from feathers, cloth, masks, and jaguar skins mounted on light cane supports.

Bright Cloth

The modern Mayan woman below wears a traditional woven hair ribbon, 80 ft. (25 m) long. Ladies showed their rank by wearing cloth dyed with bright colors. The Maya obtained bright red dye by squeezing a cochineal bug. For purple they used the same mollusks as the ancient Romans did, but instead of killing them they rubbed two together to make them release their dye.

Rope Sandals

Mayan sandals were made from a piece of leather threaded with two cords that were passed between the wearer's front toes. Rich people decorated their sandals with feathers, shells, and disks of jade.

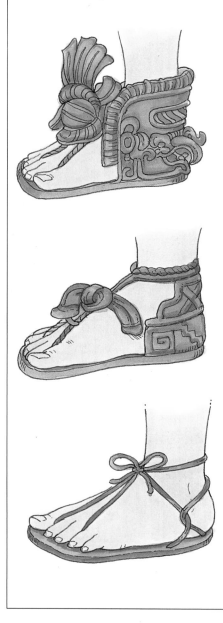

A Lord and Lady's Costume

King Shield Jaguar, left, wears a headdress, sash, sandals, and jewelry. His wife Lady Xoc wears her best *huipil*. You can see that it is woven down the sides with a border of feathers. The Maya loved brilliantly colored feathers, and there are more in her headdress. She is pulling a rope woven with thorns through her pierced tongue, to offer her blood to the gods.

Making a Feather Border

This is how to tie feathers onto a border for a cloak. You will need a board, drawing pins, strong thread, and feathers.

1 Cut a piece of thread 8 in. (20 cm) long. Pin both ends to the board. Cut a second, longer thread. Lay it beneath the first, but pin only one end.

3 Take the loose end of the second thread. Wind it around the bent quill twice and push the end through the second loop. Pull it tight.

2 Slide the point of the feather up under the top thread. Bend it over the cotton and back on itself.

4 Do the same with the next feather, sliding it close to the first. Keep doing this until you have filled the thread, then unpin and knot the cotton. Turn your border over and sew it onto the cloth.

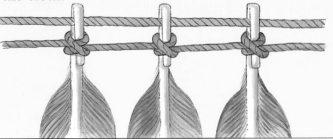

Pottery and Stone

Pots

The Maya made cooking pots, beautiful little statues, and delicate bowls from clay. They were all shaped by hand, without a potter's wheel. Some pots were covered with a glaze of red, white, or black clay and polished with a smooth stone to give a glossy, waterproof surface. Others were painted with melted wax, then covered with the colored glaze. Firing the pot burned away the wax, leaving parts of the pot plain to contrast with the glaze.

Making a Pot

1 On a flat stone the potter makes a ring of clay. She gradually adds more clay and smooths it. Instead of turning the pot on a wheel, she walks around it.

2 She shapes the neck by rolling a wet corn cob over the surface, supporting it from the inside. After smoothing the pot with a wet cloth, she leaves it to dry.

3 When the pot is hard enough, the potter turns it over. She tidies up the ragged edge and adds another roll of clay.

4 Using the corn cob, she begins to close the hole. She must make the inside as thin and smooth as possible before she closes it over.

5 Turning the pot the right way up, she wets the sides. Finally, she adds the handles.

Firing a Pot

The Maya fired their pots on an open fire of sticks and straw. This was burned for about an hour, until the ash turned light gray. The pots were left to cool slowly so that they did not crack.

Decorating a Pot

You can try a Mayan potter's decorating techniques. You will need a rolling pin, round-ended stick, pointed stick, paintbrush, knife, and clay.

1 Roll out a circle of clay for the bottom of the pot and a long strip for the sides. Wet the edges of the circle and carefully stick the strip around it. Smooth the ends of the strip together. Leave your pot until it is hard but still dark.

2 Roll up some little balls of clay. Paint a dab of water on the pot and press them on. With the round-ended stick, press in the pattern of dimples.

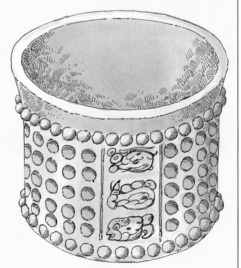

3 Use the pointed stick to draw your picture. With your knife, carefully scrape clay from the picture so that it stands out like a carving. The glyphs shown on this pot mean "His cup for his cocoa."

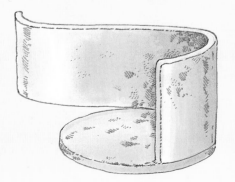

Jade

The Maya called jade the "stone of grace." It was the color of growing corn and symbolized life. The type of jade the Maya collected as pebbles and boulders from riverbeds is called jadeite, which is even harder than Chinese jade.

It seems impossible that the Maya carved such a hard stone without metal tools. The secret was in the quartz sand, which actually did the cutting. To cut a groove, they sprinkled sand on the jade surface and sawed with a piece of string. To cut out a circular core, they twirled a reed or hollow bird-bone on the sand-sprinkled surface.

A Death Mask

When he was buried in the crypt at the Temple of Inscriptions, Lord Pacal had the flesh of his face stripped off and replaced with the mask above, made of 200 pieces of carved jade.

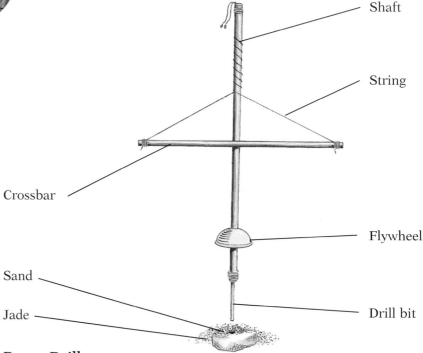

Pump Drill

To bore through a jade bead, the Maya invented the pump drill. Before drilling, the worker twirled the crossbar to wind the string around the shaft. He sprinkled sand on the jade, then stood the drill bit—a pointed stick or hollow bone—on top of it. As he pushed down on the crossbar, the string unwound, making the shaft and bit spin, grinding the sand into the jade. The pottery flywheel kept the drill steady.

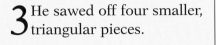

Making Earrings

Maya craftsmen made flower-shaped earrings with no waste and the fewest possible cuts. You can carefully cut up an apple with a sharp knife to show how they did this in the following stages.

1 With a hollow drill bit, the craftsman drilled out the core of a jade pebble. Using sand and string, he sawed it in half.

2 He sawed off four large pieces, one for each side.

3 He sawed off four smaller, triangular pieces.

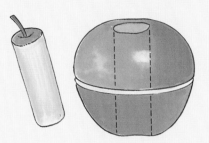

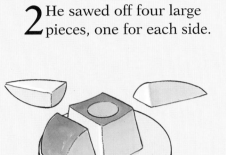

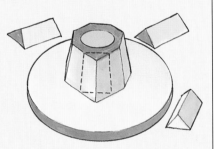

4 This left an ear flare, which was rubbed smooth.

5 He didn't waste the offcut pieces: they were turned into little pendants or beads.

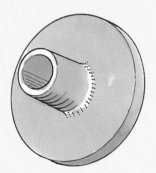

This mask of jade shows a man wearing earrings.

6 He put the earring together by threading string through the flare, the core, and the beads. A plate behind the ear counterbalanced the weight of the earring.

Stone

The Maya had no metal, but they had some materials that were almost as valuable. In the volcanic highlands they found a glassy stone called obsidian, which could be shattered into pieces with razor-sharp edges for cutting and scraping. In the lowlands, limestone contained pieces of flint, which could also be used as blades for tools. The Maya became masters of the different techniques for shaping these stones.

Pyrite

Among the most amazing stone ornaments the Maya made were plaques containing pyrite, which is a glittering, gold-colored mineral. Mayan craftsmen shaped, fitted together, and polished the pyrite and glued it onto flat disks of slate up to 10 in. (25 cm) across. Kings wearing the plaques may have stood on temple platforms, reflecting the sun from a hundred glittering surfaces.

Pyrite Disk

The Maya ground an intricate design into the slate disk for the plaque, using sand sprinkled beneath a drill of bone or wood. The slate was stuck to the pyrite with a glue of fine clay mixed with resin.

Cross-section of pyrite disk

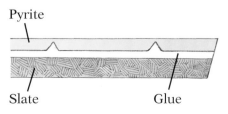

Pyrite

Slate

Glue

Eccentric flint

Craftsmen spent hundreds of hours shaping ornaments called "eccentric flints" by pressing the point of a deer antler against the edge of the flint. Each stroke flaked off a thin, shell-shaped fragment. This eccentric flint shows the silhouette of two people in headdresses.

This picture of the flint from above shows the thickness of flint broken off with each blow.

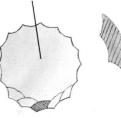

Flint Blades

Mayan workers used various techniques for making different types of flint blades. By striking the flint with a hard stone or pressing a wooden tool against it, the worker could flake off small blades for making into arrowheads. Here, the worker is using a stone hammer and a punch, made from an antler, on a piece of flint. The punch breaks off large blades from the flint that is held in the worker's lap.

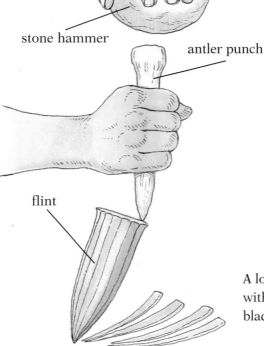

stone hammer

antler punch

flint

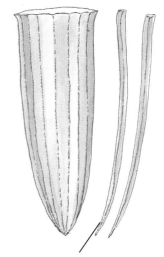

A long, thin blade of flint is removed with each blow of the punch. The blades are all about the same size.

Travel and Trade

Each part of the Maya lands produced different goods: salt, shells, and fish on the coast; cotton, corn, and flint in the lowlands; copal incense, rubber, and feathers in the tropical forests; jade in the region around Quirigua on the Montagua River; obsidian and granite in the highlands. Merchants carried these goods hundreds of miles to exchange in the city markets.

For money, the Maya used cacao beans from the cacao tree that grew along riverbanks. Dishonest traders made counterfeit coins by stripping the husks of the beans, filling them with sand, and mixing them with genuine beans. Careful customers squeezed each bean to test it. They did all their math by laying the beans on the ground.

Litters

The wealthy merchant shown on this pot is being carried in a litter. It is made from basketwork and jaguar skin, lashed onto two wooden carrying poles.

Dugout Canoes

Wherever they could, traders went by water. They paddled huge dugout canoes around the coasts or along inland rivers. The Maya made their dugout canoes by felling hardwood trees and chopping out the insides with razor-sharp flint axes. Flat wooden paddles were bound with rawhide to give the rowers a better grip.

Carrying Basket

Because they had no pack animals, the Maya had to carry everything on their own backs. This Mayan painting shows a scene from a fishing village on the coast. If you look closely, you can see fish being dried in one of the houses, which are thatched and raised on platforms. In each of the top corners, you can see a figure carrying a heavy basket supported by a strap around his forehead.

Writing

The Maya wrote thousands of books, of which only four are left. The Spanish who invaded Central America in the sixteenth century burned the rest. Luckily, the Maya also painted and carved inscriptions on pots, walls, and pillars.

The Maya made paper from the bark of the fig tree. The papermaker first stripped the bark from the tree. The inner bark was then wrapped in fresh banana leaves and steamed over a fire of green logs. It became damp and soft and turned from green to yellow. Stone "bark beaters" were used to stretch the bark thinner and up to five times its original width. The surfaces of the beaters were grooved to help knit the bark fibers together. The last beater had the finest grooves, which made the paper very smooth. As the paper dried, it turned reddish brown. To make a good writing surface, the papermaker coated it with a thin layer of plaster.

Writing Materials

This sculpture shows a woman writing in a codex. Mayan scribes wrote with brushes of soft animal hair, using paint pots made from conch shells cut in half. The bark pages of the codex were stuck together in a long strip, folded like a screen and covered with jaguar skin.

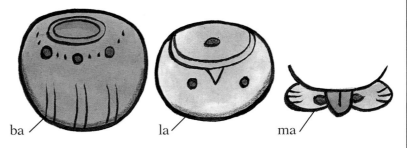

Glyphs

The Maya wrote by using pictures or symbols, called glyphs. They used two types of glyphs. The first showed a picture of the thing described. The glyph on the left shows a jaguar's head and means "balam," which was the Mayan word for jaguar.

ba   la   ma

The second type of glyph used pictures that each represented a different sound. These sounds could be put together to form the syllables of a word. The last vowel of the last syllable was always cut off. So, these three pictures combine to mean "ba-la-m," or jaguar.

By putting these pictures together, the Maya could create a single glyph like the one below that also meant "balam," or jaguar.

ba

la

ma

Codex Page

This page from one of the four remaining Mayan books is painted in red, blue, and black on the white plaster-coated surface. It shows a god with a firestick, beneath the glyphs at the top of the page. It was part of a calendar that predicted good and bad days.

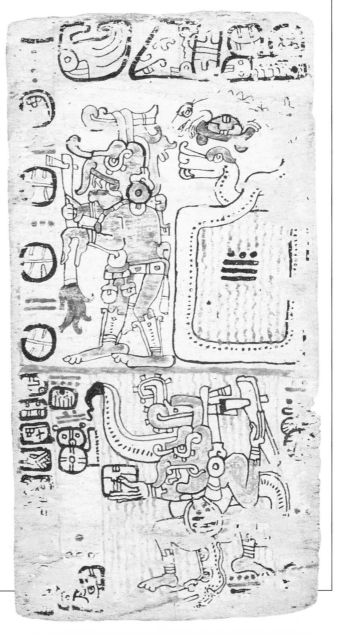

Numbers

The Calendar Round

This diagram shows how the Maya combined the Sacred Almanac and Vague Year to create a Calendar Round of 18,980 days, each with its own name. Very few people lived more than the fifty-two years of one Calendar Round.

The Maya used several different calendars. Their Sacred Almanac of 260 days, the length of a human pregnancy, was for organizing religious ceremonies. Their Vague Year of 365 days was used for farming. A calendar called the Long Count began on August 13, 3114 B.C., the date that the Maya thought the world began. It measured the *kin* (days), *uinal* (months of twenty days), *tun* (years of eighteen months), *katun* (twenty years), and *baktun* (400 years) that had passed since that date.

These two wheels show the Sacred Almanac. The small wheel with thirteen numbers turns against the big wheel with twenty day names. This gives the date as 8 *Ahau*.

This wheel with 365 segments shows the Vague Year. It is divided into eighteen months of twenty days, plus a five-day period called "The Sleep." This calendar shows the thirteenth day in the month called *Ceh*.

The three pictures that line up give the combined name of the date in the Calendar Round as 8 *Ahau*, 13 *Ceh*.

Counting

In Mayan numbers, a dot represented one and a bar represented five. Traders used cacao beans and sticks to show dots and bars, with a shell meaning zero.

0	1	2	3	4	5	6	7	8	9

10	11	12	13	14	15	16	17	18	19

Mayan Arithmetic

In our decimal system the value of each place to the left increases by the power of ten. The Maya worked from bottom to top and in twenties. A dot on the baseline meant 1, on the next line 20, on the third 400 (20 x 20), and on the fourth 8,000 (400 x 20). A bar meant 5 on the bottom line, 100 on the second, 2,000 on the third, 40,000 on the fourth. To add or subtract, the Mayan traders laid their cacao beans (dots), sticks (bars), and shells (zeros) on the right lines. A shell represented zero. Can you figure out the missing values of these Mayan numbers? (The answer is on page 45.)

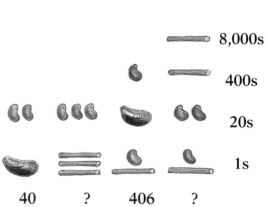

8,000s

400s

20s

1s

40   ?   406   ?

Watching the Stars

The doorways around the observatory at Chichen Itza point to the setting sun and moon at special times of the year. Using a simple pair of notched sticks, Mayan astronomers calculated that the moon took an average 29.53 days to complete its cycle, predicted eclipses, and calculated the year on Venus as 584 days, within one-tenth of a day of its true length.

Music

The first thing you might notice about the instruments on this page is that none of them has strings. The Maya made their music with drums, trumpets, rattles, and whistles. We know that music was important. In battle scenes, Mayan painters show musicians adding the noise of their long wooden trumpets to the din. At religious festivals, musicians played for dances in honor of the gods.

Conch Shell Trumpet

Trumpets were made by cutting the tips off conch shells. Drilling holes into them created a range of different notes. This incense burner was made in the shape of a figure, covered in tattoos, blowing a conch shell trumpet.

Drums

This painting from a codex shows two musicians beating on drums made by covering hollow logs with animal hide. The hide was stretched over the log while wet and became a tight drum skin as it dried. The drum was called a *huehuetl*. Perhaps it made a sound like its name. Other Mayan percussion instruments included maracas, made by filling a dry gourd with stones, and a turtle shell covered with stretched hide.

Making pan pipes

People of Central America made pan pipes out of lengths of bamboo, sawing them across with sharp obsidian blades and burning out the knots inside. You can use thin, smooth plastic piping like garden hose. You will also need strong twine, a sharp knife, and some clay.

1 Cut your hose into eight lengths, making each length about .02 in. (0.5 cm) shorter than the one before.

2 Cut carefully around each mouthpiece, making the edge as sharp as you can.

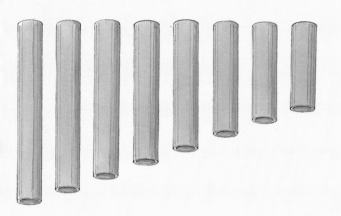

3 Lay the pipes side by side with the mouthpieces in a straight line and bind them together with the twine. Twist the twine between each pipe.

4 Stick a lump of clay in the end of each pipe, closing the hole completely. Blow across the top of each pipe until you get a note.

5 Make the note of a pipe lower by pushing the clay down, higher by pushing it up. Experiment until you can play a scale.

Health and Beauty

Mayan doctors knew that some diseases were infectious and recognized the symptoms of many illnesses. Most of their medicines were made from plants boiled into syrups or made into ointments. We know of more than 400 Mayan prescriptions. Tests have shown that many of these would have been very effective. For example, they used wild poppy sap, which contains opium, as a sedative; allspice, which has a local anesthetic, for toothache; and castor oil for constipation.

Chili Peppers

Mayan doctors mashed roasted chili peppers (right) with honey to spread on wounds to stop infection. They also boiled chilies into a tea for curing earaches, bowel problems, and chest infections. Recent experiments show that chilies are high in vitamin C. They contain capsaicin, which can relieve headaches, and may be effective against food poisoning, gangrene, botulism, and tetanus.

Strange Cures

Here are two of the many strange cures used by Mayan doctors.

1. To extract a tooth easily, burn alive a yellow-throated iguana. Test the ashes by rubbing them on one of your dog's teeth. If the tooth pulls out easily, use them on your own tooth. If it doesn't, try the ashes of a green-throated iguana (left).

2. To help relieve stuffiness when you have a cold, put a few borage leaves in a cup, fill with boiling water, and add a teaspoonful of honey. Let it stand for five minutes, strain, and drink.

Flattening Skulls

The Maya used technology to change their own appearance as well as their surroundings. They tied boards to the front and back of newborn babies' heads for a few days to flatten the soft bones of the skull and make the forehead slope. Mothers hung beads in front of their babies' noses to make their eyes cross, which was also thought to be a mark of beauty.

This carving shows a man and woman with flattened heads, which were considered beautiful by the Maya. The Maya also liked to have an attractive smile, which meant painful visits to the dentist. He bored small holes into people's teeth with an obsidian-tipped drill, then inserted tiny jade stones.

41

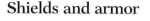

Warfare

By looking at the paintings and sculptures that kings made to celebrate their victories in battle, we can tell how the Maya fought. They had two aims: to defeat a neighboring state and to take prisoners. Those who died in battle were luckier. Captives, especially of high rank, were taken home to be paraded in public before they were sacrificed to the gods.

Shields and armor

Mayan weapons and armor are vividly shown on this mural that decorates a temple wall at Bonampak. Both warriors wear headdresses of woven cane and feathers and fight with thrusting spears. The man on the right wears a sleeveless tunic of jaguar skin. This was stuffed with cotton and soaked in saltwater. It stiffened as it dried, forming body armor to deflect a spear's blow. The other warrior uses a shield of woven cane covered in leather. The man in the center has been taken captive, an important part of Mayan battles.

The *Atlatl*

Until the Maya began to use bows and arrows, the *atlatl* was the best weapon for shooting missiles fast and accurately from a distance.

The warrior laid a wooden dart with a sharpened point hardened in fire along the atlatl and put two fingers through the holes. He put his arm back as far as he could and then thrust forward, shooting his dart.

Making Face Stamps

To make themselves look fierce, warriors used stamps to apply patterns to their faces. They made stamps by carving clay when it was leather hard and then baking it.

1 You can make a face stamp by cutting a large potato in half and carving out a pattern. This Mayan stamp shows the number nine (a bar and four dots), but you could make up a pattern of your own.

2 Dip the potato pattern into some face paint, then press it against your cheek.

Scars and Tattoos

Men and women decorated their skin by cutting it with an obsidian knife to make raised scars, sometimes rubbing in dye to create tattoos. You can see the scars above this ferocious warrior's nose. He also wears a magnificent headdress made from cane and feathers.

Technology Through Time

It is not clear when the people we call the Maya came into existence. They may have been descended from the Olmec civilization, which existed in Central America from around 1200 to 400 B.C. The Classic Period of the ancient Maya lasted from A.D. 250 to 925. During this period, the Mayan people used and developed the technology that is described in this book.

3000–1800 B.C.	People live in the Maya region by gathering seeds and roots and by fishing and hunting. Their wooden spears are tipped with flaked obsidian blades and thrown with *atlatls*. As the climate grows warmer, turning grassland to desert, and game becomes overhunted, they have to depend more on vegetables and begin to cultivate corn, beans, and chili peppers. They use hollowed-out gourds to store food and water.
1800–1000 B.C.	On the Pacific coast of Guatemala, people settle in small villages, building mud-walled houses. They plant fields, using wooden digging sticks. They use stone *metates* and *manos* for grinding corn.
1700 B.C.	Inhabitants of the Mayan region begin to use cooking pots. They weave baskets, mats, and ropes but probably have not learned to spin cotton. They flake obsidian into blades and make stone axes.
1000–300 B.C.	The main villages grow into cities with rulers living in palaces on platforms. Craftsmen produce jade jewelry. Cotton is spun and woven on backstrap looms. The Olmecs, who mave been ancestors of the Maya, probably create the Long Count calendar.
600 B.C.	The first signs of Mayan writing.
300 B.C.–A.D. 250	Writing, bar-and-dot numbers, and the Long Count calendar become widespread. The Maya build stepped pyramids with stone carvings. Farmers work in raised fields alongside canals dug to drain the land.

0 B.C.	The first recorded crowning of a king.
A.D. 250–925	The Classic Period of Mayan technology.
A.D. 292	The first recorded Long Count date, carved at Tikal.
C. A.D. 400	The Long Count disappears. In the main cities huge temples, palaces and ballcourts are built and rebuilt. Metates are made with tripod legs. The Maya make books of bark paper. Bone is made into needles and drills for grinding jade. Musical instruments are made of bone, gourds, conch shells, and wood.
A.D. 800	The frescoes at Bonampak are painted.
A.D. 909	The last recorded date in the Classic Period. The great cities are abandoned and fall into ruins.
A.D. 1528	1528 The Conquest of Yucatan by the Spanish begins. They enslave and convert the Maya, who rise against them repeatedly in the following centuries.

Puzzle Answer

The answers to the puzzle on page 37 are 75 and 42,046.

Glossary

Amino acids Chemicals in the body that form protein.

Aristocracy The highest class, or nobility, of a society.

Cisterns Tanks for storing water.

Codex An ancient book.

Counterfeit Forged, not genuine. For example, false money.

Eclipses Movement of the planets where one blocks out the light from the other.

Glyph A picture or symbol used to represent a word.

Incense A gum that gives off a sweet smell when burned. Often used in incense holders during religious ceremonies.

Latex A milky fluid found in trees, particularly the rubber tree.

NASA National Aeronautics and Space Administration. The agency responsible for the exploration of space.

Ochre A mineral containing clay used as a pigment, varying in color from yellow to brown and red.

Peccary A wild animal, similar to a pig.

Porous Allowing water to pass through.

Quetzal A bird prized by the Maya for its dazzling green tail feathers. It is also the word for the highest value of money in Guatemala.

Rain forests Forests in tropical areas with heavy rainfall.

Resin A substance found in plants such as the gum tree. It is used to make glue.

Sarcophagus A stone coffin, often decorated with sculpture and inscriptions.

Slip A creamy mixture of clay and water used to decorate pottery.

Tapir A hoofed animal with a flexible snout.

Wicker Twigs braided and woven together.

Further information

Books to read

Baquedano, Elizabeth. *Aztec, Inca and Maya* (Eyewitness). New York: Knopf Books for Young Readers, 1993.

Chrisp, Peter. *The Maya* (Look Into the Past). Austin, TX: Thomson Learning, 1994.

Greene, Jaqueline D. *The Maya* (A First Book). Danbury, CT: Franklin Watts, 1992.

Hooper-Trout, Lawana. *The Maya* (Indians of North America). New York: Chelsea House, 1991.

Meyer, Carolyn and Charles Gallenkemp. *The Mystery of the Ancient Maya*, revised edition. New York: Margaret McElderry Books, 1994.

Sherrow, Victoria. *The Maya Indians* (Junior Library of American Indians). New York: Chelsea House, 1993.

Acknowledgments

Many thanks to Jamie Marshall at The Guatemalan Indian Center for all his assistance.

The pictures in this book were kindly supplied by AKG London 29, 35, 38, 41; Bruce Coleman /J. Cancalosi 30, 40(bottom), /S. Widstrand 40(top); © K. Deuss, The Guatemalan Indian Center, London 11(top), 20, 21, 22, 24, 27; C. M. Dixon 25, 32; Werner Forman Archive *cover* (background), 1, 4, 16, 17, 18, 19, 23(bottom), 31, 34, 43; Robert Harding 8, 23(top); Michael Holford 15, 37; National Museum of Anthropology, Mexico City 28; © Mireille Vautier 9, 13, 33, 42; Wayland Picture Library 11(bottom). All artwork is by Peter Bull Art Studio except for Christa Hook *cover*, 14; Stephen Wheeler 5, 6(left), 35.

Illustration: Peter Bull Art Studio
Cover illustration: Christa Hook

Index

Page numbers in **bold** indicate that there is information about the subject in a photograph or diagram.